God's Plan
and the
Overcomers

God's Plan
and
The Overcomers

WATCHMAN NEE

Translated from the Chinese

Christian Fellowship Publishers, Inc.
New York

Available from the Publishers at:

11515 Allecingie Parkway
Richmond, Virginia 23235

TRANSLATOR'S PREFACE

Does God have a plan? If so, what is His plan? How will it be carried out? Are we involved in it? And is there any opposition? These are not mere speculative questions, for the right understanding of them is vital to our spiritual well-being.

In this present volume Watchman Nee lays before us the eternal plan of God, which is, to sum up all things in Christ that Christ might have the preeminence in all things (Eph. 1.10, Col. 1.18). This plan is violently opposed by Satan who unjustly seeks that place for himself. Though temporarily the Adversary appears to succeed in frustrating God's plan, nevertheless at the appointed time God sends His own Son into the world to destroy all the works of the devil and to remove all obstacles to His plan. It is on the cross that Christ has accomplished the work of redemption, and He now calls His church to stand in His victory and work together with Him in bringing all things under His feet. Yet due to the failure of the church, the responsibility falls upon the overcomers of the church. And through the cooperation which they give to Him, Christ will realize God's plan.

What the reader will now find in the pages to follow is a synopsis of a series of messages given by the author at a conference held in Shanghai, China, in 1934. It was published in this outline form in the issues of the early years of *Revival* magazine. The original manuscript of the full text, which contained over 100,000 words, was destroyed during political upheavals in China—hence permanently lost. However, the message is so vital and relevant to our time that the synopsis is now being translated for the first time into English for the benefit of those in the English-speaking world who seek to know the mind of God and to walk before Him as overcomers.

CONTENTS

Scripture quotations are from the
American Standard Version of the Bible
(1901), unless otherwise indicated.

PART ONE

GOD'S PLAN

God's Plan

Thou art the Christ, the Son of the living God.
(Matt. 16.16)

Christ is all, and in all.(Col. 3.11)

In all things he might have the preeminence.(Col.
1.18)

The mystery of God, even Christ.(Col. 2.2)

For we preach . . . Christ Jesus as Lord.(2 Cor. 4.5)

The Meaning of Centrality

Why are there all things? Why the angels? Did
God create all these accidentally? Or were they created according to God's plan?

Why does·God choose men, send prophets, give the
Savior, bestow the Holy Spirit, build the church and
establish the kingdom? Why does He cause the gospe!
to be preached to the ends of the earth that sinners

might be saved? Why must we reach sinners and build up believers?

Some people elevate baptism, speaking in tongues, withdrawal from sects, holiness, keeping of the Sabbath, or whatever as being central. What, though, is God's center?

God works with a definite goal in mind. Yet what is the goal of our labor? We need to have vision before we can have the goal of labor. Unless we see the centrality of God our work will be without aim.

The truths of God are all organically related. There is a center towards which all truths are focused.

Some may decide on the centrality of their work according to personal inclination and circumstantial need. But the predetermination and need of God ought to be our center.

What is the centrality of God? What is the thread that is woven through all the truths of God? What is God's overall truth?

Who is the Lord Jesus? We all might answer that He is our Savior. Yet very few can answer as Peter, who said that He is "the Christ of God" (Luke 9.20).

The center of God's truths is Christ. The centrality of God is none other than Christ—"The mystery of God, even Christ," wrote Paul. A mystery is that which is hidden in God's heart. Never before had God told anyone why He created all things, including mankind. For a long time it remained a mystery. Later on, however, God revealed this mystery to Paul so that he might explain it. And this mystery, explained the apostle, is Christ.

The Lord Jesus is the Christ of God as well as the Son of God. At the time of conception the angel Gabriel told Mary that the child to be born is the Son of God (Luke 1.35), whereas at the hour of birth an angel of the Lord announced to the shepherds that the child newly born is Christ the Lord (Luke 2.11). Peter acknowledged Jesus as both Christ and Son of God (Matt. 16.16). By His resurrection from the dead Jesus Christ our Lord is declared to be the Son of God (Rom. 1.4). By the same token He has been made both Lord and Christ by God (Acts 2.36). In believing Jesus as Christ and as Son of God men may have life in His name (John 20.31). In himself, so far as His own place in the Godhead is concerned He is the Son of God. But in God's plan and according to God's work the Lord Jesus is God's Christ because He is anointed by God. From eternity to eternity, He is the Son of God. He becomes Christ as far back as when the plan of God was laid. The purpose of God is centered on His Son, "that in all things he might have the preeminence"; the plan of God is also centered upon His Son so that Christ might be "all in all" (Col. 1.18, 3.11).

God created all things and mankind for the sake of manifesting His glory. Today believers are manifesting a little something of Christ. But one day all things shall manifest Christ because the whole universe shall be filled with Him. In creating all things God desires that all things will manifest Christ. In creating man He wishes that man should be like His Son, having the life of His Son and possessing the glory of His Son in order that His only begotten Son might be the first-born among His many sons. The reason for God to create and to redeem man is all for the sake of Christ. Redemption is undertaken in order to achieve the aim of creation. Christ is the bridegroom, and we are the bride. He is the chief corner-stone, and we are the many living stones of the building. God created us so as to satisfy the heart of Christ. As we see the relationship of Christ with us, we give thanks. As we see the relationship of God with Christ, we offer praises. The centrality of God is indeed Christ, for all the purpose of God is centered upon Him. Now there are two aspects to God's purpose: (1) that all things might manifest the glory of Christ, and (2) that man might be like Christ, having both His life and glory.

ONE: CHRIST IN ETERNITY PAST

Christ Has the Preeminence in God's Plan

SCRIPTURES ON GOD'S PLAN:

And to make all men see what is the dispensation of the mystery which for ages hath been hid in God who created all things; to the intent that now unto the principalities and the powers in the heavenly places might be made known through the church the manifold wisdom of God, according to the eternal purpose which he purposed in Christ Jesus our Lord.(Eph. 3.9–11)

Which he made to abound toward us in all wisdom

and prudence, making known unto us the mystery of his will, according to his good pleasure which he purposed in him unto a dispensation of the fulness of the times, to sum up all things in Christ, the things in the heavens, and the things upon the earth; in him, I say, in whom also we were made a heritage, having been foreordained according to the purpose of him who worketh all things after the counsel of his will.(Eph. 1.8–11)

Worthy art thou, our Lord and our God, to receive the glory and the honor and the power: for thou didst create all things, and because of thy will [or, *pleasure—AV*] they were, and were created.(Rev. 4.11)

Yet to us there is one God, the Father, of whom are all things, and we unto him; and one Lord, Jesus Christ, through whom are all things, and we through him. (1 Cor. 8.6)

For of him, and through him, and unto him, are all things. To him be the glory for ever. Amen. (Rom. 11.36)

Even before the creation of the world, God has a plan. This plan is made in Christ, and that plan is to sum up in Christ all things which are in the heavens and on the earth. God plans all of this out of the good pleasure of His will. God is Number One. So that all things are of Him and through Him.

SCRIPTURES ON GOD'S PLAN IN GIVING ALL THINGS TO CHRIST:

He that descended is the same also that ascended far

above all the heavens, that he might fill all things. (Eph. 4.10)

The Father loveth the Son, and hath given all things into his hand.(John 3.35)

Jesus, knowing that the Father had given all things into his hands, and that he came forth from God, and goeth unto God.(John 13.3)

All things whatsoever the Father hath are mine: therefore said I, that he taketh of mine, and shall declare it unto you.(John 16.15)

Now they know that all things whatsoever thou hast given me are from thee.(John 17.7)

[God] hath at the end of these days spoken unto us in his Son, whom he appointed heir of all things, through whom also he made the worlds. (Heb. 1.2)

In eternity past God has predetermined to establish a house over which the second person in the Godhead, the Son, shall rule. He has given all things to the Son as His inheritance. All things are of the Son, through the Son, and to the Son. The Father plans, the Son inherits whatever the Father has planned, and the Holy Spirit accomplishes all that the Father has planned. The Father is the Planner, the Son is the Heir, and the Holy Spirit is the Executor. The love of the Father towards the Son commences in eternity past. He is the Beloved of the Father. Even in eternity the Father has loved the Son. When the Son comes to the world the Father still declares, "This is my beloved Son" (Matt. 3.17). The Father loves the Son and has given all things into His hands. As the Son faces death He knows that the Father has given all things into His hands (John 13.3). His resurrection and ascension are for the sake of filling all things (Eph. 4.10).

TWO: CHRIST IN CREATION

Christ Has the Preeminence in the Creation of All Things and Mankind

SCRIPTURES ON THE CREATION OF ALL THINGS BY CHRIST:

Through him also he made the worlds [literally, *ages*]. (Heb. 1.2)

And upholding all things by the word of His power.(Heb. 1.3)

In the beginning was the Word, and the Word was with God, and the Word was God. The same was in the beginning with God. All things were made through him; and without him was not any thing made that hath been made.(John 1.1–3)

He was in the world, and the world was made through him, and the world knew him not.(John 1.10)

For in him were all things created, in the heavens and upon the earth, things visible and things invisible, whether thrones or dominions or principalities or powers; all things have been created through him, and unto him;

> and he is before all things, and in him all things con-
> sist. (Col. 1.16,17)
>
> One Lord, Jesus Christ, through whom are all things,
> and we through him.(1 Cor. 8.6)

The Father having conceived the plan, the Son proceeds to create. The Father plans according to His good pleasure, the Son approves and creates, and the Holy Spirit energizes for its accomplishment. The Son is the Creator of all things, He is "the firstborn of all creation" (Col. 1.15), and He has the preeminence over all things. He is "the beginning [literally, *chief*] of the creation of God" (Rev. 3.14). For God in His eternal plan has predetermined before the foundation of the world that the Son shall create all things and then become flesh to achieve redemption (1 Peter 1.18–20). Hence in God's plan the Son is the head of all creation. The Father plans and the Son creates. And after the work of creation is done, all creation is given to the Son. The reason for creating all things is to satisfy the heart of the Son. Oh how great is our Lord! He is the Alpha and the Omega. He is the Alpha, because *of* Him are all things. He is the Omega, for *unto* Him are all things.

SCRIPTURES ON THE CREATION OF MAN BY CHRIST:

> But I would have you know, that the head of every
> man is Christ; and the head of the woman is the man;
> and the head of Christ is God.(1 Cor. 11.3)

But when the fulness of the time came, God sent forth his Son, born of a woman, born under the law, that he might redeem them that were under the law, that we might receive the adoption of sons. And because ye are sons, God sent forth the Spirit of his Son into our hearts, crying, Abba, Father. So that thou art no longer a bond-servant, but a son; and if a son, then an heir through God. (Gal. 4.4–7)

Even to them that are called according to his purpose. For whom he foreknew, he also foreordained to be conformed to the image of his Son, that he might be the firstborn among many brethren: and whom he foreordained, them he also called: and whom he called, them he also justified: and whom he justified, them he also glorified.(Rom. 8.28–30)

According to the foreknowledge of God the Father. (1 Peter 1.2)

God is faithful, through whom ye were called into the fellowship of his Son Jesus Christ our Lord.(1 Cor. 1.9)

For not unto angels did he subject the world to come, whereof we speak. But one hath somewhere testified, saying, What is man, that thou art mindful of him? Or the son of man, that thou visitest him? Thou madest him a little lower than the angels; thou crownedst him with glory and honor, and didst set him over the works of thy hands: thou didst put all things in subjection under his feet. For in that he subjected all things unto him, he left nothing that is not subject to him. But now we see not yet all things subjected to him. But we behold him who hath been made a little lower than the angels, even Jesus, because of the suffering of death crowned with glory and honor, that by the grace of God he should taste of death for every man. For it became him, for whom are all things, and through whom are all things, in bringing many sons unto glory, to make the author of their salvation perfect through sufferings.(Heb. 2.5–10)

Wherefore let no one glory in men. For all things are yours; whether Paul, or Apollos, or Cephas, or the world, or life, or death, or things present, or things to come; all are yours; and ye are Christ's; and Christ is God's.(1 Cor. 3.21–23)

God creates man in order for man to be like Christ, having the life as well as the glory of Christ. As God manifests himself through Christ, so the latter manifests himself through man. God calls us in order that we might become partakers of His Son, being made to be conformed to the image of His Son so that His Son might become the firstborn among many brethren. From eternity past up to the resurrection the Lord is the only begotten Son. But after He is raised from the dead He becomes the firstborn Son. Accordingly, after the resurrection He says this to Mary Magdalene: "Go unto my brethren, and say to them, I ascend unto my Father and your Father" (John 20.17). These many sons become sons in the only begotten Son. By the death of God's only begotten Son, many sons are born.

But God causes us to be heirs as well as sons. He gives us the life of His Son. He also makes us co-heirs with His Son. The Son came to be man, being made a little lower than the angels; but He is later on crowned with honor and glory. He is to lead many sons into glory. The reason why God creates man is that man may receive the life of His Son and enter into glory with His Son. All is to satisfy the heart of His Son. Let us thank God, because He creates us and redeems us for the sake of satisfying the heart of Christ.

God has foreordained that man be conformed to the image of His Son. (The foreordination of God is according to His foreknowledge. Such foreordination is related to our future destiny. Election is concerned with us as men. Thus foreordination is for us in eternity, whereas election and calling is for us in this age.) What is the meaning of being conformed to the image of His Son? God takes His Son as the mold or stamp, and in this stamp God impresses us many sons so that His Son might be the firstborn among many sons. He causes us to have the glory of His Son as well as the life of His Son (Rom. 8.29–30). He motivates His Son to lead many sons into glory. The Son of God is "he that sanctifieth", we are the "they that are sanctified", and the "all of one" signifies our being of the one Father; "for which cause he is not ashamed to call them brethren" (Heb. 2.10,11). Christ is now in us, for the purpose of making us sons of God. In the future He will lead us into glory. No wonder we read this: "Christ in you, the hope of glory" (Col. 1.27). Today we are the children of God, and in the future we shall enter into glory with Christ (Rom. 8.16,17). It is the will of God to distribute the life of His Son to many so as to enable many to become sons of God in order that His Son may become the firstborn among many sons so that His Son might have the preeminence in all things.

There is a difference between the personal Christ and the corporate Christ. 1 Corinthians 12.12 speaks of the corporate Christ which is the composite of the personal Christ and the church. There the term Christ (or more accurately: *the Christ*, Darby) refers to the church. We were all born in Adam, but today we are all in Christ since we have His life. Adam is the first man, but Christ is the second man as well as the last Adam (1 Cor. 15.47,45). Before His death and resurrection there is only the one personal Christ. But after His death and resurrection He distributes His life to many, thus forming the corporate Christ.

SCRIPTURES ON WHAT GOD HAS FOREORDAINED **BEFORE** THE FOUNDATION OF THE WORLD:

Father, I desire that they also whom thou hast given me be with me where I am, that they may behold my glory, which thou has given me: for thou lovedst me before the foundation of the world.(John 17.24)

Even as he chose us in him before the foundation of the world, that we should be holy and without blemish before him in love: having foreordained us unto adoption as sons through Jesus Christ unto himself, according to the good pleasure of his will.(Eph. 1.4, 5)

In hope of eternal life, which God, who cannot lie, promised before times eternal.(Titus 1.2)

Who saved us, and called us with a holy calling, not according to our works, but according to his own purpose and grace, which was given us in Christ Jesus before times eternal, but hath now been manifested by the appearing of our Saviour Christ Jesus, who abolished death, and brought life and immortality to light through the gospel.(2 Tim. 1.9, 10)

Who was foreknown indeed before the foundation of the world, but was manifested at the end of the times for your sake.(1 Peter 1.20)

God laid His plan before the foundation of the world. He loved the Son before the foundation of the world. He has foreordained the Son to be Christ. He has chosen us for sonship (Election is choosing us as men; foreordination is giving us sonship.). Before times eternal God gave us grace. He has foreordained that we should partake of His life (not His deity). God foreknew how Satan would rebel and cause all things to be at variance with Him. He also foreknew how man would sin and fall. God therefore held council with His Son even before the foundation of the world so as to have His Son come down and go to the cross in order to reconcile all things back to himself, rescue fallen mankind, and resolve the rebellion of Satan.

SCRIPTURES ON WHAT GOD HAS FOREORDAINED **FROM THE** FOUNDATION OF THE WORLD:

Then shall the King say unto them on his right hand,

Come, ye blessed of my Father, inherit the kingdom prepared for you from the foundation of the world. (Matt. 25.34)

For we who have believed do enter into that rest; even as he hath said, As I sware in my wrath, they shall not enter into my rest: although the works were finished from the foundation of the world.(Heb. 4.3)

Else must he often have suffered since the foundation of the world: but now once at the end of the ages hath he been manifested to put away sin by the sacrifice of himself.(Heb. 9.26)

And all that dwell on the earth shall worship him, every one whose name hath not been written from the foundation of the world in the book of life of the Lamb that hath been slain [or, *the Lamb slain from the foundation of the world*—mg.].(Rev. 13.8)

... they whose name hath not been written in the book of life from the foundation of the world ... (Rev. 17.8)

The realization of God's plan commences from the foundation of the world. The Lord is the Lamb slain from the foundation of the world. Our names were written in the book of life from the foundation of the world. God's works of creation were finished from the foundation of the world. God's eternal kingdom was also prepared from the foundation of the world.

THREE: CHRIST IN ETERNITY TO COME

Christ Has the Preeminence in Eternity

SCRIPTURES ON THE CONDITIONS IN ETERNITY AFTER
REDEMPTION:

Wherefore also God highly exalted him, and gave unto him the name which is above every name; that in the name of Jesus every knee should bow, of things in heaven and things on earth and things under the earth, and that every tongue should confess that Jesus Christ is Lord, to the glory of God the Father.(Phil. 2.9–11)

Worthy art thou, our Lord and our God, to receive the glory and the honor and the power: for thou didst create all things, and because of thy will they were, and were created.(Rev. 4.11)

Worthy is the Lamb that hath been slain to receive the power, and riches, and wisdom, and might, and honor, and glory, and blessing. And every created thing which is in the heaven, and on the earth, and under the earth, and on the sea, and all things that are in them, heard I saying, Unto him that sitteth on the throne, and unto the Lamb, be the blessing, and the honor, and the glory, and the dominion, for ever and ever. And the four living creatures said, Amen. And the elders fell down and worshipped.(Rev. 5.12–14)

Beloved, now are we children of God, and it is not yet made manifest what we shall be. We know that, if he shall be manifested, we shall be like him; for we shall see him even as he is.(1 John 3.2)

Blessed be the God and Father of our Lord Jesus Christ, who according to his great mercy begat us again unto a living hope by the resurrection of Jesus Christ from the dead, unto an inheritance incorruptible, and undefiled, and that fadeth not away, reserved in heaven for you.(1 Peter 1.3, 4)

And he showed me a river of water of life, bright as crystal, proceeding out of the throne of God and of the Lamb, in the midst of the street thereof. And on this side of the river and on that was the tree of life, bearing twelve manner of fruits, yielding its fruit every month: and the leaves of the tree were for the healing of the nations. And there shall be no curse any more: and the throne of God and of the Lamb shall be therein: and his servants shall serve him; and they shall see his face; and his name shall be on their foreheads. And there shall be night no more; and they need no light of lamp, neither light of sun; for the Lord God shall give them light: and they shall reign for ever and ever.(Rev. 22.1–5)

After Christ had died and been raised from the dead, "God highly exalted him, and gave unto him the name which is above every name; that in the name of Jesus every knee should bow, of things in heaven and things on earth and things under the earth, and that every tongue should confess that Jesus Christ is Lord . . ." For "God hath made him both Lord and Christ" (Acts 2.36), and has "put all things in subjection under his feet" (Eph. 1.20–22). Revelation 4 and 5 show us the glorious and blessed state of the Lord after His resurrection and ascension. In chapter 4 it is recorded that all the created things praise God for His creation. Chapter 5 records that they praise God for His redemption. God shall put all enemies under the feet of Christ (Matt. 22.44). In this particular task the church bears great responsibility today, because God is waiting for the church to fulfill this mission.

The whole creation was subjected to vanity (Rom. 8.20) after the rebellion of Satan and the fall of man ("vanity" means failure of the result designed, losing the original purpose, having no more direction). Today all things are subjected to vanity, waiting for the manifestation of the sons of God. During this waiting period all things are under the bondage of corruption (such as the diminishing of sunlight, the dying of wood and grass, and so forth). However, the creation has an earnest expectation to be delivered one day from this bondage of corruption. For this reason the whole creation groans and travails in pain together until now. When the children of God enter into the liberty of glory, all things shall be liberated. The day our body is redeemed all things shall be set free. Nevertheless, even now we can foretaste the powers of the age to come (Heb. 6.5)—(the church foretastes the powers of the age to come, and the kingdom age foretastes the powers of eternity). In the future our body will be redeemed, and we will receive sonship and enter into the liberty of glory (Rom. 8.19–23).

When the Lord shall appear we will be like Him (1 John 3.2). We will be sons with God's life and nature; but we will also be heirs, having God's inheritance and glory.

Revelation 21 and 22 describe the situation in eternity, not in the millennial kingdom. There are four significant points in these two chapters: (1) God; (2) the Lamb; (3) the city—with its inhabitants who are the foreordained ones before the foundation of the world, the thirsty ones mentioned in Revelation 7 who shall thirst no more; and (4) the nations. God and the Lamb are the center of the city. Revelation 21.9–21 describes the city, whereas 21.22–23 speaks of the center of the city. The glory of God is the light, and the Lamb is the lamp thereof. As light is magnified through a lamp, so God is magnified by the Lamb. The center of the new creation is the city, New Jerusalem, the sons of God; and the center of this city is God and the Lamb. The glorious light of God is in the Lamb. The Lamb lightens the city, and the light of the city enlightens the nations. The city has only one street and one river (no one shall ever lose his way since there is but this one street). Evidently the street winds up like a coil. The river is located in the midst of the street and flows along with the street. Both the street and the river proceed out of the throne of God and of the Lamb, hence God and the Lamb are the center. "And when all things have been subjected unto him, then shall the Son also himself be subjected to him that did subject all things unto him, that God may be all in all" (1 Cor. 15.28).

We are shown that the aim and purpose in whatever God does from eternity to eternity is to give the Son the preeminence in all things. For the purpose of God is to make His Son the Lord of all.

FOUR: CHRIST IN REDEMPTION

Christ Has the Preeminence in Redemption

The aim behind God's plan is twofold: (1) that all things might manifest the glory of Christ so that Christ could have the preeminence in all things; and (2) that man might be like Christ, having both His life and glory. Colossians chapter 1 informs us of these very aspects—namely, (1) that in all things Christ might have the preeminence (v.18), and (2) that Christ is the head of the church (v.18). Ephesians chapter 1 also tells us the same thing, (1) to sum up all things in Christ, both things in the heavens and things upon the earth (v.10), and (2) that in Christ also, the church is made a heritage (v.11). Revelation 4 and 5 likewise describe these two sides, telling us (1) what becomes of all the created things, and (2) what becomes of the redeemed.

God creates to accomplish His plan. He created all things and man with the intent that all things might manifest Christ, especially man—who would be like Christ, having His life and glory. But Satan rebelled and brought in such an interference that all things became discordant and man fell into sin. God reacted with redemption in order to regain the purpose of His creation. Consequently, the redemption of Christ must (1) reconcile all things to God, and (2) redeem fallen mankind by imparting His life to man. It also needs to solve two of God's problems—(1) solve the rebellion of Satan, and (2) resolve the sin of man. In total, then, the redemption of Christ is aimed at settling these four matters: to realize God's double purpose of reconciling all things back to himself and giving His life to man, and to resolve God's twin problems of the rebellion of Satan and the sin of man. The first two of these four are positive and affirmative, whereas the other two are negative in nature.

Christ's Redemption Realizes God's Double Purpose

Before the foundation of the world the Father and the Son held a council, the result of which was that the Son was to come to the world as a man for the sake of accomplishing the work of redemption. Hence redemption was not God's contingent measure but on the contrary was an action which had been foreplanned. Moreover, we can see from this that it is not a case of Christ coming to the world to be a man after the likeness of Adam, for it must be noted that Adam was created after the image of Christ. Genesis 1.26 lays down the plan of God, while Genesis 1.27 describes God's execution of the plan. Verse 26 says "let us" plan, verse 27 is its execution: "created man in his own image"; verse 26 reveals the council of the Godhead, verse 27 tells of the creation of man in the image of the Son. Only the *Son* in the Godhead has an image. Accordingly, Adam was created after the image of Christ. Adam is "a figure of him [Christ] that was to come" (Rom. 5.14). The coming of Christ to this world was not an emergency act; it came out of the foreplan of God. Even before the foundation of the world, Christ was anointed. Christ is a universal man who is not restricted by time and space. He was the Anointed before the foundation of the world, and He is the Christ who fills the universe. The Four Gospels view Christ as the universal man.

The first event in the redemption of Christ is His birth. In becoming a man He steps down from the position of the Creator to the place of the created. By taking upon himself the body of the created He is able to die for man and for all things. With Bethlehem there can be Calvary. With the manger there can and will be the cross.

(1) The redemption of Christ is to reconcile all things to God. Since all things were created in Christ (Col. 1.16), God is able to deal with all things when He deals with Christ. In Christ, therefore, all things have been dealt with by God. Just as Levi paid tithes when still in the loins of Abraham (Heb. 7.9,10), so all things tasted death in Christ (Heb. 2.9 reads: ". . . so that by the grace of God he should taste death for every *thing*"—Darby). On the cross He reconciles all things to God (Col. 1.20). The scope of the redemption of Christ reaches not only to mankind but to all things as well. All things—they not having sinned—need not be redeemed but need simply to be reconciled.

(2) The redemption of Christ imparts His life to man. In the work of redemption Christ not only reconciles all things to God but also gives life to man that the latter might be like Him. This is the release of His

life. While He was on earth His divine life was imprisoned within His physical body and thus was greatly restricted. While He was in Jerusalem He could not be in Galilee. His death, though, sets His imprisoned life free.

The grain of wheat mentioned in John 12.24 is God's only begotten Son. The life of the wheat is hidden inside the husk. If it does not fall into the ground and die, it abides alone. But if it dies, the husk is decomposed and the inner life is liberated so as to bear many grains. Each one of the many grains resembles the first grain. Yet it can also be said that each one of the grains is in that one grain. Christ dies to beget us. Before death He is the only begotten Son. After resurrection He becomes the firstborn Son among many sons. By the resurrection of Christ God begets us and gives us His life.

The "fire" mentioned in Luke 12.49 is the life of Christ. During His days on earth His life was straitened within His body. Through baptism, that is to say, through the death of the cross, His restricted life was set free. So that after His life was liberated it was cast upon the earth. Since that day when it was cast upon the earth it has been kindled. Hence the death of Christ is the great emancipation of the life of Christ! Through His death He distributes His life to us.

Christ's Redemption Resolves God's Twin Problems

We have just seen how the redemption of Christ realizes the double purpose of God. Now we will see how it resolves God's twin problems.

(1) *The redemption of Christ solves the problem of Satan's rebellion.* It is not just the cross of Christ that overcomes Satan; it is His blood. Satan well knew that if he could inject his poison into the first married pair, this poison would propagate itself in all who would be born by them. Consequently, Satan and our forefathers committed spiritual fornication by which the lying poison of sin entered the soul of our forefathers. Since the soul life is in the blood (see Lev. 17.11 mg.), therefore this sinful human life has been reproduced throughout the generations ("he made of one blood every nation of men"—Acts 17.26 Stephens' *Greek Text*, 1550). The sinful poison injected into the first couple has flowed into our life through the blood.

The blood of Christ contains no poison. It is the precious blood and is incorruptible. On the cross He bore the sins of many and poured out all His blood in death. When Christ was raised from the dead He had no blood. After His resurrection He has bones and flesh but no blood, "because he poured out his soul unto death" (Is. 53.12). In Christ our blood has already been poured out. Hence Satan has no more ground of operation in our lives. The blood of Christ has destroyed and finished Satan and all who are his.

(2) *The redemption of Christ also resolves the problem of the sin of man.* Our sins require the death of Christ. His substitutionary death dismisses our criminal case before God. His representative death delivers us from the dominion of sin.

Thus, the death of Christ realizes God's double purpose and at the same time resolves God's dual problem. This is the victory of Christ. And this victory is already won. God leaves us on earth to maintain this victory and to proclaim throughout the whole creation concerning this victory (Col. 1.23). In baptism and the breaking of bread we perform and exhibit the victory of the death of Christ before the holy angels and the evil spirits, before the nations and the whole creation.

The Purpose of Redemption

The purpose of the redemption of Christ is to make us a people for His own possession (Titus 2.14) that we might be a living sacrifice to Him (Rom. 12.1): living and dying for Him (Rom. 14.7-9, 2 Cor. 5.15) and serving as the Temple of the Holy Spirit to glorify God (1 Cor. 6.19,20)—so that Christ might be magnified in us whether by life or by death, because for us to live is Christ (Phil. 1.20, 21).

The aim of redemption is to let Christ have the preeminence in all things. In order to have this first place in all things, Christ must first have the preeminence in us. And why? Because we are the firstfruits of all creation (cf. James 1.18). After *we* are in subjection to Christ, all *other* things will follow in subjection. The cross works in our lives to enable God to realize this aim in us. Is it not the cross that decreases us and increases Christ? The cross seeks out for Christ the place of preeminence. God uses the cross, which in turn works through circumstances to dig deeply into our lives so as to make us know Christ

mend our rent. The lack of patience speaks of the lack of Christ. Instead, God intends to let Christ have the preeminence in all things. Putting self to death is not holiness. Holiness is Christ. Christ himself must have the first place in all things!

Should God give us power it will only make us powerful persons instead of Christ having the preeminence in our lives. But with Christ as our power He has the first place in us. The reason why we do not have power is because we are not weak enough. For the power of Christ "is made perfect in weakness" (2 Cor. 12.9). It is not Christ making me powerful; it is Christ being power unto me!

Hudson Taylor saw the truth of the matter in the phrase, "ye are the branches" (John 15.5). The writer of the booklet *The Life That Wins* (Charles Trumbull) discovered that Christ is the victory. Not drawing on the power of Christ to help me live, but letting Christ himself live in me! Not Christ giving me power to be patient, but letting Christ be "patient" out from me! "Lord, I allow You to love out through me!" Not overcome by the help of Christ, but let Christ himself overcome! Not I overcome by Him, rather He overcomes through me. With faith I commit myself to the Lord and let Him live out His own self through me. Not I live by the help of Christ, but "Christ liveth in me" (Gal. 2.20). I live by the life of Christ, and I also live by "the faith of the Son of God" (Gal. 2.20 Darby). When we believe and receive the Son of God, not only His life but His faith too enters into us. Hence we may live by *His* faith.

Christ is victory! Christ is patience! What we need is not patience or gentleness or love, only Christ. He must have the preeminence in all things. Christ lives out patience, gentleness and love through us. What do we deserve but death. We are not fit for anything but death. When God created Adam He gave the latter a command to keep. Yet God does not *re*-create us in the same fashion. He instead puts us in the place of death while He himself lives out His will in us. We should not only see that there is a Savior who died in our stead on Calvary, but even more so realize that this same One lives in us and for us now. He is made by God to be "our wisdom": to be both our "righteousness" for the past that we might be saved, our "sanctification" for the present that we might live a holy life, and our "redemption" for the future that our body might be redeemed (1 Cor. 1.30 mg.). Thus He indeed has the preeminence in all things!

How We Enter into This Victorious Life

We must:

(1) Be fully despaired of ourselves. We need to know ourselves so thoroughly that we see ourselves as fit for nothing but death. We must come to the end of any life in ourselves. For our extremity is God's opportunity. As long as we still have life in ourselves we are not able to accept the victory of Christ. Christ is already dwelling in us, except that He is not given the place to rule in us.

(2) Be completely consecrated. There needs to be

definite and specific consecration. Unless we see the utter weakness of ourselves we will not accept the cross and completely surrender all our managing powers to the Lord.

(3) Believe. Having consecrated ourselves, we must believe that Christ has already taken up government over us and is now living through us.

As Christ lived in the flesh which Mary gave to Him, so He is to live through our flesh. He is living today on earth by our flesh exactly as He once lived on earth in His own flesh. He is to live in our lives. Our victory is based on letting Christ have the preeminence in all things—in allowing Him to be the Lord of all to our lives.

The Old Testament tells us how the chosen people of God lived on earth. At first the tabernacle served as the center of the twelve tribes; later it was the temple which became their center. The center of the temple was the ark. The tabernacle, the temple and the ark are all types of Christ. As long as the children of Israel maintained their proper relationship with the tabernacle or the temple they were victorious, and no nation could overcome them. Even though their enemies learned how to fight while they themselves were not familiar with fighting, the children of Israel overcame all their enemies nonetheless. But the moment they had problems with the tabernacle or the temple, they were taken into captivity. Nothing else—whether they had powerful kings or great wisdom in themselves—mattered at all; the only concern which mattered was whether or not they had offended the ark of the tabernacle or temple. If the Lord had the preeminence, then theirs was the victory. So, too, with us today. In minding the victory of Christ, we also have the victory. But whenever the hair of separation is shorn, the victory is gone (cf. Judges 16.17). Except we give Christ the highest place we are not able to overcome. Unless Christ has the preeminence in our heart we cannot overcome.

Christ Has the Preeminence
in the Experience of a Christian

SCRIPTURE TO BE READ:

He must increase, but I must decrease.(John 3.30)

The experiences of a Christian are of two kinds: the sweet and the bitter. God leads us through both the sweet and the bitter experiences of life in order to enable us to let Christ have the preeminence in all things.

A. Sweet Experiences

(1) *Prayer answered*—Prayer will be answered if it aims at letting Christ have the first place in all things. Seek first the kingdom of God and His righteousness, and God will add to us all our needs. (Adding is not giving. The first means adding to what is al-

ready there; the second means giving what is not there.) Asking in the name of the Lord is asking the Father for the Lord so that the Lord himself might receive it. According to this principle they who mind the flesh will have nothing for which to pray. How we need to let the cross cut off our flesh that we might be the Lord's intercessors praying out the Lord's will. We should not pray for our selfish purposes. Only those who permit Christ to have the preeminence in all things can enter the Holiest of all. May we transform the time of praying for *our* needs into a time of praying for God's affairs. God will then hear the prayer we have uttered—that is, prayer for the things of God; but He will also hear the prayer we have not uttered—that is, prayer for our own affairs. If we would ask first that the Lord might receive His, He would cause us to receive ours too. One of the sweet experiences in the life of a Christian is to have prayer continually answered. Remember, though, that the reason for God answering our prayer is to allow Christ to occupy first place in all things.

(2) *Growth*—Growth is also a sweet life experience of the Christian. We should be childlike, but not remain children. The increase of knowledge of the Holy Scriptures is not growth; the increase of Christ in us is growth. Less of self, even none of self, is growth. Think little of ourselves—nay, think nothing of ourselves—and that is growth. For instance, true humility is a not looking at oneself at all. Seeing oneself produces relative humility, but a not looking at oneself at all yields absolute humility; and that is

growth. Growth is letting Christ have the preeminence in my life: "He must increase, but I must decrease"—yet He is not increased in me according to how much scriptural knowledge I have, but according to how far my consecration is. In the measure of my putting myself in God's hand will be the measure of my having Christ preeminent in all things. Real growth is in magnifying Christ.

(3) *Enlightenment*—Another sweet experience of a Christian life is receiving light from God, that is to say, spiritual vision. Revelation is what God gives us—an objective giving. Light is what God makes us see in revelation—a subjective seeing. Vision is what we see when God's light shines upon us: it includes both light and revelation. First the enlightenment, then the faith. If we desire to be enlightened continually we must always let Christ have the preeminence in all things. "If therefore thine eye be single, thy whole body shall be full of light" (Matt. 6.22). We are unable to understand, not because things are not understandable but because our eyes are not single. "Blessed are the pure in heart: for they shall see God" (Matt. 5.8). The heart must be pure. "If any man willeth to do his will, he shall know . . ."(John 7.17). Only those who allow Christ to have the preeminence in all things will receive light.

(4) *Power*—Having power is also one of the sweet experiences in the Christian life. To have power, one needs to let Christ sit on the throne of his life. As *He* increases, the person has power. Without separation there can be no power. Separation is not only a com-

ing out but is also an entering into—that is, an entering into Christ. What distinguishes the Christian from the world is the fact that he belongs to Christ and is clothed with Christ: Christ is his power.

B. Bitter Experiences

(1) *Material loss*—Generally speaking, believers seem to have financial difficulties. This is due either to their inability to continue on with whatever improper occupations they had engaged in before or to some spiritual reasons for which God is dealing with them specifically. God sometimes takes our wealth away so as to induce us to seek after Christ that He might have the preeminence in all things. It is not *impossible* for the rich to enter the kingdom of God, it is just *difficult* for them to do so. Not that they cannot serve the Lord, only that they find it difficult to serve the Lord. "Lay thou thy treasure in the dust . . . and the Almighty will be thy treasure" (Job 22.24,25). God dealt with the children of Israel in the wilderness by depriving them of earthly supplies of food and clothing so that they might recognize the abundance of God. As the supplies on earth ceased, the supplies from heaven came. Material difficulties drive us to seek after the Lord, to learn the lesson of faith, and to know Christ as the first in all things. Whenever difficulty arrives let us believe that it comes from God, and rejoice. Yet never *expect* difficulty, because Satan is well able to add such to us.

(2) *Emotional anguish*—In the loss of parents, husbands, wives, children, relatives and friends God is drawing us to find in Christ our satisfaction. God deprives us of these relationships in order that we might accept Christ as Lord and let Him have the preeminence in our lives. It is not because God desires to ill-treat us but because He wants us to take Christ as our Lord. It is more precious to shed tears before the Lord than to be joyful before men. What we find in the Lord is that which we would not find in parents, wives and children. In the realm of creation God's dealing with believers is for the one reason of giving His Son the preeminence in all things. By offering Isaac, we gain Isaac. God will not allow us to have anything outside of His Son.

(3) *Physical pain*—God permits us to be sick and weak in body that we may learn to (1) pray in the night, (2) watch as the sparrow on the housetop, (3) know how the Lord makes our bed, (4) deal with sins, (5) wait in stillness, (6) touch the hem of the Lord's garment, (7) realize how God sends His word to heal us, (8) discern how God uses sickness to make us useful vessels, (9) understand that holiness is healing, and (10) experience the power of the Lord's resurrection in overcoming our weakness, sickness and death. God causes us to learn through sickness how to believe, trust, and obey so that Christ can have the preeminence in our lives.

(4) *Agony over natural virtues*—How people still depend on their own natural virtues even after they are saved! Yet as days go by, perhaps after a few

years, the Lord will take away their natural virtues, thus causing them deep agony. He will strip us of our Adamic virtues and show us our depravity. The reason for such deprivation is to fill us with Christ.

In conclusion, then, whatever God gives us—whether sweet or bitter—is to induce us to let Christ have the preeminence in our lives.

SIX: CHRIST IN THE WORK AND MESSAGE OF A CHRISTIAN

Christ Has the Preeminence in the Work and Message of a Christian

Life and experience are inward, while work and message are outward. Christ must have the preeminence not only inwardly but also outwardly. Hence Christ must have first place in the believer's work and message.

SCRIPTURES TO BE READ:

> For we are his workmanship, created in Christ Jesus for good works, which God afore prepared that we should walk in them.(Eph. 2.10)
> For I determined not to know anything among you, save Jesus Christ, and him crucified.(1 Cor. 2.2)
> For we preach not ourselves, but Christ Jesus as Lord, and ourselves as your servants for Jesus' sake. (2 Cor. 4.5)

Christ Has the Preeminence
in the Work of a Christian

Christ should have the first place in our work—"For good works, . . . that we should walk in them" (Eph. 2.10). Christ *is* good works, since the very aim of all God's work is Christ. We therefore ought to walk in such works. Leaving aside the fact of our daily occupations, we are all doing God's work; hence we should walk in the good works of God.

Serving God and working for God are vastly different. Many work for God, but they are not serving Him. Faithful works—if they are really for Christ—are judged by motive and purpose. Doing God's work has its pleasure as well as its pain. Though there is hardship, there also is ease. It possesses its own interest and attraction. Oftentimes we work for interest and not for Christ. Many rush here and there to gain fame in works. They have indeed done some works, but in reality they have not served God. God works from eternity to eternity for the sake of giving His Son the preeminence in all things. Therefore we too must work for Christ. Unless God cleanses our motive and intent, we cannot be blessed of Him. We work for Christ, not for sinners. The measure of our success in work is determined by the measure of Christ in our works. Oh, at the very start of a work may we allow the Holy Spirit to lay open the thoughts and intents of our heart so that we are enabled to discern if it is of the spirit or of the soul.

We must not labor for our own increase, for our own group, or even for our own pet teaching; we ought to work solely for Christ. We rejoice if God can gain something. We are glad whenever He has something to gain even though it does not come from our work. We are not out to save our teaching but to save sinners. Not out to gratify our own heart, simply to satisfy the heart of Christ. In case we prosper and gain, the Lord will be hindered and will suffer loss. Were we to be content with God's gain we would be delivered from pride and jealousy.

Frequently we seek our own glory as well as the glory of God. God saves souls for the sake of Christ, not for our own sake. Paul planted and Apollos watered. The work was not done by one person—lest people would say, I am of Paul, or, I am of Apollos. The whole approach of work is for Christ and not for the workers. We are as bread in the Lord's hand. After people have eaten, they thank the One who gives bread and not the bread itself—which is, us. From start to finish the work is all for Christ, never for ourselves. We are content with the work and position which our Lord has appointed to us or arranged for us. We should not "glory in another's province in regard of things ready to our hand" (2 Cor. 10.16). How we like to desert our own ground and tread on another's field. The question is not whether we are able to work, but whether God has commanded us to work. Sisters, for example, need to keep their place (1 Cor. 14.34,35); they should not be teachers, that is to say, they should not be those deciding with authority the word of God (1 Tim. 2.12). In all our works we must let Christ have the preeminence.

Christ Has the Preeminence
in the Message of a Christian

Christ should also occupy the first place in our message. As those did in the early days of the church, so we today ought to preach "Christ Jesus as Lord" (2 Cor. 4.5) and to know nothing among others "save Jesus Christ, and him crucified" (1 Cor. 2.2). Christ is the center of God's purpose and plan. The cross stands at the center of God's work since it operates to fulfill His purpose. The cross works to set aside all which is of the flesh so that Christ might have the preeminence. Our central message should not be dispensation, prophecy, type, kingdom, baptism, leaving denominations, speaking in tongues, keeping the Sabbath, holiness, and so on; it ought instead to be Christ. The centrality of God is Christ. We must therefore also take Christ as our center.

After a person is saved he should be taught to consecrate himself to be a bondslave of Christ: to accept Him as his Lord of all.

The truths in the entire Bible are organically united, just like a wheel with all its spokes. The center is Christ. Not that we do not preach truths other than the central truth, but that we need to connect all the other truths to the center. We should know two things: (1) what this particular truth is—what does it talk about; and (2) what is the relation between this specific truth and the center. We ought to pay attention to the center, though this does not exclude the teaching of the other truths related to the center. After Paul had declared that he was determined "not to know

anything among you, save Jesus Christ, and him crucified", he then proceeded to say that "we speak wisdom, however, among them that are fullgrown"
(1 Cor. 2.2,6). Only after people have consecrated
themselves and have accepted Christ as their Lord are
we able to speak to them the deeper truths for edifica-
tion.

When we work we should always draw people to
the center and show them that Christ is Lord. It is impossible for us to undertake such work on a purely
objective basis. We first must be broken by God so as
to make Christ the preeminence in our lives before we
help others into accepting Christ as Lord so as to allow Him to have the first place in their lives. Unless
we live out the life of Christ as being preeminent in us,
we are unfit to preach this message to others. For we
ourselves need to be the message we would preach.
How we must let Christ have the preeminence in
small things of the day in order to preach the message
of Christ as center. Oh that each of us would put
Christ on the throne!

As long as *God's* will is done, what does it matter
if I am placed in the dust! A "good" from the Lord ex-
ceeds all the praises of the world (cf. Matt. 25.21,23;
Luke 19.17). The smiling face of heaven far surpasses
all the angry faces on earth. Heavenly comfort tran-
scends earthly tears. The hidden manna is to be en-
joyed in eternity. May the Lord so bless His word as
to win us as well as win others.

PART TWO

GOD'S OVERCOMERS

God's Overcomers

SCRIPTURE TO BE READ:

> . . . the church, which is his body, the fulness of him
> that filleth all in all.(Eph. 1.22, 23)

God's Eternal Plan

God conceived an eternal plan even before the
foundation of the world. His plan, as we have said,
serves the dual purpose of: (1) having all things to
manifest Christ, and (2) making man to be like Christ
—which is to say, for man to have the life and glory of
Christ. In realizing His dual aim, however, God en-
counters two problems: (1) the rebellion of Satan, and
(2) the fall of man.

In an earlier age an archangel became jealous,
through pride, at seeing Christ the center of all things.
He wished to exalt himself to be equal with the Son of

God. Intent on grasping for himself the centrality of Christ, he rebelled. One third of the angelic hosts followed him in rebellion against God. Even the living creatures on earth followed suit. Satan's rebellion hurled all things into chaos, it being no longer possible for them to manifest Christ. All things today may still declare the glory of God (Ps. 19.1), but they certainly cannot manifest God himself.

God therefore created man in order that (1) having the life and glory of Christ and being given dominion over all things, man might bring all things back to God; and (2) being united with God, he might be used of Him to deal with Satan's rebellion. Unfortunately, man fell.

Hence for God's dual purpose to be realized, He must now resolve these two problems. He must (1) redeem fallen mankind, and (2) eliminate Satan's rebellion.

In order to realize God's dual purpose and resolve God's twin problems, the Lord Jesus came down from heaven to become man and accomplish the work of redemption. He is the Christ of all things as well as the Christ of mankind. He is the centrality as well as the universality. Universality means that which is not limited by time and space. Christ is not only the Christ of the Jews and the Christ of the church, He is the Christ of all things. He is all, and in all.

The redemption of Christ has three cardinal features: that of (1) substitution—for the individual; (2) representation—for the church; and (3) headship—for all things. Christ is the Head, therefore He includes all. And the death of Christ is an all-inclusive death. So that just as the Federal Head died, so also all things included in the Head died too. His death as Federal Head had brought all things as well as mankind into death, thus reconciling all things and mankind back to God.

Christ has resolved every problem on the cross. There He crushed the head of the serpent. He has solved Satan's rebellion and destroyed all the latter's works. There too He redeemed the fallen race and reconciled all things to God. Through the cross He imparts His life to men that they might be like Him.

In sum, by the cross Christ has realized God's double purpose and resolved God's two great problems.

The Position and Responsibility of the Church

What position does God give the church? What is the vision God entrusts to the church on earth? Why does He permit Satan, whose head is already crushed, to remain on earth?

God leaves the church on earth not only to preach the gospel to save sinners but also to demonstrate the victory of Christ on the cross. He permits Satan to remain on earth for the sake of creating opportunity for us to prove the victory of His Son. He expects us to exhibit the victory of His beloved Son. Consequently, a defeated believer brings disgrace to God.

The church is the body of Christ. And the body ought to carry on the work of the Head. The church is the fullness of Christ. As Christ overflows, there is the church. The church is to continue what has already been done and taught as recorded in the Four Gospels.

There are three principal points to be found in the New Testament: (1) the cross, (2) the church, and (3) the kingdom. On the cross Christ has accomplished redemption and won the victory. The kingdom is to manifest the redemption and victory which Christ has achieved. But in the meanwhile the church is now to maintain on earth that which Christ has fulfilled on the cross. The cross speaks of God's legal judgment. The kingdom is to reveal the execution of God's authority and power. But the church stands between these two to affirm what the cross has accomplished and to foretaste the powers of the kingdom age to come (cf. Heb. 6.5).

Satan cannot overcome the personal Christ. Yet he is able to put the personal Christ to shame through the corporate Christ—because the defeat of the body is construed to be the defeat of the Head. And the failure of one of its members is taken as the failure of the whole body. We are the complement of Christ ("... he shall see his seed, he shall prolong his days ..."—Is. 53.10), just as formerly we were the extension of Adam. God leaves us on earth for the sake of our fulfilling His eternal plan and arriving at His purpose of the ages.

Before the ark was brought into Jerusalem it remained in the house of Obed-Edom (2 Sam. 6). May we faithfully guard the blood—the work of Christ, and the cherubim—the glory of God, which are both connected with the ark.

The Nature of Christ's Victory and the Church

SCRIPTURE TO BE READ:

> He that overcometh, I will give to him to sit down
> with me in my throne, as I also overcame, and sat down
> with my Father in his throne.(Rev. 3.21)

The victory of Christ is the pattern for all victories
—"As I also overcame . . ."

Three Enemies

The Bible tells us we have three different enemies:
(1) *the flesh*—in us, (2) *the world*—outside of us, and
(3) *Satan*—above and below us. According to the ascended position of the church, Satan is under us.

The Old Testament uses three different tribes to
typify these enemies. The Amalekites typify the flesh,
which is to be overcome through constant prayer. The
Egyptians signify the world, which needs to be buried
in the Red Sea. And the Caananites represent the
powers of Satan, which must be conquered and destroyed one by one.

The flesh is set against the Holy Spirit: "the flesh
lusteth against the Spirit, and the Spirit against the
flesh; for these are contrary the one to the other"
(Gal. 5.17). The world opposes the Father: "If any
man love the world, the love of the Father is not in
him" (1 John 2.15). And Satan contends with Christ:

"To this end was the Son of God manifested, that he might destroy the works of the devil" (1 John 3.8). We thus see that the flesh is overcome by walking after the Holy Spirit; the world is overcome by loving the Father; and Satan is overcome by believing in Christ.

The first enemy that appears is the flesh. In the earlier era an archangel became self-centered and willed to exalt himself to be equal with God. This is how self first entered the world. This marks the beginnings of sin, the world, and Satan.

When God created man He gave the latter a tremendous power, that of reproduction. Man is able to pass on his life to his progeny. Originally God had the hope that man would eat the fruit of the tree of life, thus possessing God's life and transmitting the same to his descendants. Accordingly, He forbade man to eat the fruit of the tree of the knowledge of good and evil. Satan slipped in and committed spiritual adultery with this first couple. He injected his poisonous seed into them for them to reproduce it in their descendants. Satan is the father of liars (John 8.44). His seed is the lie, whereas God's seed is the truth. The principle with which Satan tempted Adam to sin is the same principle on which he himself sinned.

Satan has his kingdom as well as his family. He gets people to become children of his family and to be citizens of his kingdom over whom he then acts as king.

After Satan had tempted man to sin his operation thereafter was confined to the earth, that is to say, to the world. The curse he received was that "upon thy belly shalt thou go, and dust shalt thou eat all the days of thy life" (Gen. 3.14). He can rule, walk on the earth, and take man—who came out of dust—as his food. Accordingly, this is Satan's great defeat. Even in the fall of man God has won a tremendous victory.

Satan has his organization on earth, and what he organizes becomes the world. He is king in his own organized world, and the whole world lies under him (1John 5.19).

The Victory of Christ

Before the Lord Jesus came forth for public ministry He was first baptized. This signifies that it was in death and resurrection that He carried on the work of three years and a half. There was absolutely no flesh involved in the work of *His* life. We call the life of these three and a half years a life of the cross. The Lord Jesus never did anything according to His own will. He always did the will of Him by whom He was sent. He not only did the Father's will, He also waited for the Father's time (John 7.6,10).

In tempting the Lord, Satan tried to entice Him to act outside of the word of God—to entice Him, for example, to turn stone into bread. But the Lord answered, "Man shall not live by bread alone, but by every word that proceedeth out of the mouth of God" (Matt. 4.4). He frequently said, "The Son can do nothing of himself, but what he seeth the Father doing" (John 5.19); and, "I can of myself do nothing:

as I hear, I judge" (John 5.30). "Of himself " means a coming out of himself, that is, a drawing upon himself as the source. Satan often tempts people to verify themselves after they have been validated by God. How he lures the Lord to prove himself to be the Son of God after God has already borne witness to this fact (at His baptism).

The Lord's crucifixion is wholly in accordance with God's will. For He prayed thus in the garden: "Nevertheless, not as I will, but as thou wilt"; and, "My Father, if this cannot pass away, except I drink it, thy will be done" (Matt. 26.39,42); and finally, in speaking to Peter He said, "The cup which the Father hath given me, shall I not drink it?" (John 18.11) His being able to accept the cross is victory. Unshaken by outward and inward forces, this is victory. No flesh activating itself within, no worldly attraction or instigation stirring without, and no Satanic ground being yielded to beneath—*that* is victory. Throughout His life our Lord never lived according to the flesh. He had set the flesh so completely aside that He was the first man in whom Satan had absolutely nothing. Neither the flesh nor the world nor the devil had any place in Him.

God's Desire: For the Church to Live Out the Victory of Christ

In saving men God saves them from the flesh, the world, and Satan. He calls us to deny everything which comes out of the world, what is earthly; to deny everything which emanates from self, what is of the flesh; and to deny everything which proceeds from Satan. Satan uses the world and the flesh to assault us. Only in those who are truly spiritual will Satan attack directly. Those who wholly reject the world as a system and deny the mind of the flesh will be directly assailed by Satan.

The cross of Christ needs the body of Christ. If sinners only accept the cross *objectively,* they alone will gain. But if in addition sinners receive the cross *subjectively,* God too will gain. The cross of Christ acts like a sword which cuts off all which is of the old creation from us; the resurrection of Christ gives us a new beginning.

The victory of Christ includes: (1) crucifixion—the putting away negatively all belonging to the old creation, (2) resurrection—the bringing in positively of a new beginning, and (3) ascension—the obtaining of a victorious position.

Through the death, resurrection, and ascension of Christ the church is to live out His victory on earth. The cross ought to be planted in the center of our life. God holds us responsible for letting the cross cut off all the old creation known to us (but not, incidentally, for what we are unconscious of).

WHO GOD'S OVERCOMERS ARE

SCRIPTURES TO BE READ:

He that hath an ear, let him hear what the Spirit

saith to the churches. He that overcometh, to him will I give to eat of the tree of life, which is in the Paradise of God.(Rev. 2.7)

He that hath an ear, let him hear what the Spirit saith to the churches. He that overcometh shall not be hurt of the second death.(Rev. 2.11)

He that hath an ear, let him hear what the Spirit saith to the churches. To him that overcometh, to him will I give of the hidden manna, and I will give him a white stone, and upon the stone a new name written, which no one knoweth but he that receiveth.(Rev. 2.17)

And he that overcometh, and he that keepeth my works unto the end, to him will I give authority over the nations.(Rev. 2.26)

He that overcometh shall thus be arrayed in white garments; and I will in no wise blot his name out of the book of life, and I will confess his name before my Father, and before his angels.(Rev. 3.5)

He that overcometh, I will make him a pillar in the temple of my God, and he shall go out thence no more: and I will write upon him the name of my God, and the name of the city of my God, the New Jerusalem, which cometh down out of heaven from my God, and mine own new name.(Rev. 3.12)

He that overcometh, I will give to him to sit down with me in my throne, as I also overcame, and sat down with my Father in his throne.(Rev. 3.21)

The Failure of the Church

The reason for the church to remain on earth is to

maintain and demonstrate the victory of the cross of Christ by binding Satan in every place, just as the Lord himself—the Head of the church—bound Satan at Calvary. On the cross the Lord has already judged Satan according to God's law. Now God entrusts to the church the task of executing that judgment on earth.

Knowing well how the church would affect his defeat, Satan began to persecute and kill the church. He later changed his tactics to deceive the church with falsehood. He is a liar as well as a murderer. Yet the church fears neither his smiling face nor his angry face. The book of Acts is a record of life out of death for the church. God utilized the attacks of Satan to demonstrate through the church the victory of Christ. Unfortunately, the church gradually failed—as shown in such instances as the lie of Ananias and Sapphira, the greediness of Simon, the creeping in of false brethren, the seeking by many believers of their own things, and the forsaking by many of the imprisoned Paul.

God Looks for Overcomers

Now whenever the church fails, God finds a few in the church—called to be overcomers—that they might bear the responsibility which the church as a whole ought to but fails to bear. He chooses a company of the faithful few to represent the church in the demonstration of the victory of Christ. He has His overcomers in all the seven periods of the church (as represented by the seven churches described in Revelation chapters 2 and 3). This overcomer line is never cut. The overcomers are not some special class. They are simply a group of people who conform to the *original* plan of God.

The Principle of Overcomers

The way God works, as illustrated in His Holy Scriptures, is to find a few as a nucleus in order to reach the many. This was true in the patriarchal age. At that time God chose people individually: those such as Abel, Enoch, Noah, and Abraham. Later on through Abraham (the few) God reaches the whole nation of Israel (the many)—that is to say, God reaches the dispensation of the law through the patriarchal age. Then from the dispensation of the law (the nation of Israel) God reaches to the dispensation of grace (the church out of all nations); and likewise from the dispensation of grace He will reach to the dispensation of the kingdom (the entire world), and from the dispensation of the kingdom to the new heaven and the new earth (the new creation), for the kingdom is the prologue to the new heaven and the new earth. So then, the principle of God's operation is from the few to the many.

". . . the Head, from whom all the body, being supplied and knit together through the joints and bands, increaseth with the increase of God" (Col. 2.19). The joints are for supplying, while the bands are for knitting. The Head holds the body together through these joints and bands. And these joints and bands are the overcomers.

Jerusalem typifies the whole church, whereas Zion —which is in Jerusalem—represents the overcomers in the church. Jerusalem is larger than Zion, yet Zion is the stronghold of Jerusalem. What answers to the heart of God is called Zion; that which speaks of the failure and sins of the Jews is called Jerusalem. God allows Jerusalem to be trodden down, but He usually keeps Zion intact. There will be a new Jerusalem, but there is no new Zion because Zion never grows old.

Each time the relationship between Zion and Jerusalem is mentioned in the Old Testament we are shown that the characteristics, life, blessing and establishing of Jerusalem are invariably derived from Zion. The elders were in Jerusalem, the ark was to be in Zion (1 Kings 8.1). God does good in His good pleasure to Zion, and He builds the walls of Jerusalem (Ps. 51.18). God's name is in Zion, while His praise is in Jerusalem (Ps. 102.21). God blesses out of Zion, and Jerusalem receives the good of it (Ps. 128.5). The Lord dwells in Jerusalem, yet He receives praises out of Zion (Ps. 135.21). God speaks first to Zion, and then the good tidings reach Jerusalem (Is. 41.27). He dwells in Zion and thus sanctifies Jerusalem (Joel 3.17).

God today is seeking, among the defeated church, 144,000 (a representative figure, to be sure) to stand on mount Zion (Rev. 14.1). Each and every time, He uses relatively few believers as channels to pour forth life into the church for her revival. As their Lord did, these few must pour forth blood in order to let life flow. The overcomers are to stand on the ground of victory for the church and instead of the church. They are to endure sufferings and shames.

Therefore, God's overcomers must forsake all self-complacencies, pay the cost, let the cross cut off all that comes out of the old creation, and stand against the gates of Hades (Matt. 16.18).

Are you willing to hurt your own heart that you may gain God's heart? Are you ready to let yourself be defeated so that the Lord may triumph? When your obedience is made full, God will quickly avenge all the disobedience (2 Cor. 10.6).

What the Work of the Overcomers Is

SCRIPTURES TO BE READ:

> And Joshua spake unto the priests, saying, Take up the ark of the covenant, and pass over before the people. And they took up the ark of the covenant, and went before the people.(Josh. 3.6)

> And thou shalt command the priests that bear the ark of the covenant, saying, When ye are come to the brink of the waters of the Jordan, ye shall stand still in the Jordan.(Josh. 3.8)

> And it shall come to pass, when the soles of the feet of the priests that bear the ark of Jehovah, the Lord of all the earth, shall rest in the waters of the Jordan, that the waters of the Jordan shall be cut off, even the waters that come down from above; and they shall stand in one heap. (Josh.3.13)

And when they that bare the ark were come unto the Jordan, and the feet of the priests that bare the ark were dipped in the brink of the water, (for the Jordan overfloweth all its banks all the time of harvest,) that the waters which came down from above stood, and rose up in one heap, a great way off, at Adam, the city that is beside Zarethan; and those that went down toward the sea of the Arabah, even the Salt Sea, were wholly cut off: and the people passed over right against Jericho. And the priests that bare the ark of the covenant of Jehovah stood firm on dry ground in the midst of the Jordan; and all Israel passed over on dry ground, until all the nation were passed clean over the Jordan.(Josh. 3.15–17)

For the priests that bare the ark stook in the midst of the Jordan, until everything was finished that Jehovah commanded Joshua to speak unto the people, according to all that Moses commanded Joshua: and the people hasted and passed over. And it came to pass, when all the people were clean passed over, that the ark of Jehovah passed over, and the priests, in the presence of the people.(Josh. 4.10, 11)

And Jehovah spake unto Joshua, saying, Command the priests that bear the ark of the testimony, that they come up out of the Jordan. Joshua therefore commanded the priests, saying, Come ye up out of the Jordan. And it came to pass, when the priests that bare the ark of the covenant of Jehovah were come up out of the midst of the Jordan, and the soles of the priests' feet were lifted up unto the dry ground, that the waters of the Jordan returned unto their place, and went over all its banks, as aforetime.(Josh. 4.15–18)

Always bearing about in the body the dying of Jesus, that the life also of Jesus may be manifested in our body. For we who live are always delivered unto death for Jesus' sake, that the life also of Jesus may be manifested in our mortal flesh. So then death worketh in us, but life in you.(2 Cor. 4.10–12)

The Work of the Overcomers

In examining the principle of the overcomers we must notice two things: (1) that whenever the whole body fails, God will choose relatively few to stand for the whole body; and (2) that God calls these few to carry out His command so that through them He may later reach the many.

When God chose the children of Israel He called them all to be a kingdom of priests among the nations (Ex. 19.5,6). But at Mount Sinai they worshipped the golden calf and failed terribly. Because of this, God selected the Levites—who kept His command to be His overcomers. They were given the priesthood in lieu of all the rest of the children of Israel (Ex. 32.15-29).

When God works He first works in a few, and then through them He works to the many. In order to save the children of Israel He first saved Moses. He delivered Moses out of Egypt before He delivered the children of Israel out of Egypt. He dealt with David first, and after He had laid hold of David He liberated the children of Israel from the hand of the Philistines so that they became a great nation. Spiritual end must be reached by spiritual means. God dealt with both Moses and David to such a degree that they would not at all use the flesh to help God in accomplishing His purpose.

God first gained 12 persons, then 120—and so the church was born. The principle of the overcomers is God's calling a few to do the work for the blessing of the many. A few are called so that many might receive life. God plants the cross in the hearts of the few— causing them to accept the principle of the cross in environments as well as in their homes—thus enabling them to pour forth life to other people. God needs channels of life by which to pour out life to others.

Standing in Death That Others Might Live

God put the priests in the place of death so that the children of Israel might have a way to life. The priests were the first to step into the water and the last to come out of it. They were God's overcomers. Today God is seeking a company of people who like the priests of old will step into the water, enter into death, accept the dealing of the cross, and stand on the ground of death *first,* so as *then* to open for the church a living way. God puts us first in death for the sake of giving life to others. God's overcomers are God's pioneers.

Not that the priests were capable of accomplishing anything, but because they bore the ark. They must bear the ark and descend to the riverbed. How we should let Christ (typified by the ark) be the center.

How we should be clothed with Christ and enter the water. The feet of the priests stood on the riverbed; their shoulders bore the ark. Standing in death, they as it were uplifted Christ.

The riverbed is the place of death. Nothing at all comfortable, nothing at all appealing. Not restful, not sitting, not lying, but standing. If I live according to my ill-temper, Christ cannot live in others. But if I stand at the bottom of the river, other people will cross the Jordan to victory. Death works in me, but life works in others. In my obedience to death, life will operate in others for their own obedience to God. The death of Christ quickens His life in us. Without death there can be no life.

It was most agonizing to bear the ark at the bottom of the river, for it required great diligence. A slight carelessness and the holy God would destroy them. They stood there, watching the children of Israel pass by one by one. And so they were left to the last. Consequently the apostle declared this: "For, I think, God hath set forth us the apostles last of all . . . as the filth of the world, the offscouring of all things . . ." (1 Cor. 4.9–13). He would that others believe on the gospel, yet without his chains (Acts 26.29). Oh, let each of us ask ourselves: Do I work for fame, for prosperity, for sympathy from others? Or do I seek for life in the church of God? May we be able to pray thus: O Lord, let me die that others may live.

God says explicitly that this would not be easy; nonetheless, this is the only way towards the realization of God's eternal plan.

Remaining at the bottom of the river till all the children of God had passed over speaks of how we too cannot come out of death until the kingdom finally arrives. Fortunately Joshua (a type of Christ) at last gave the command, Come up out of Jordan. Our victorious Joshua will also call us up out of the water of death. And such will mark the beginning of the kingdom.

Many people are not disobedient, they are just not *fully* obedient; with many people it is not a not paying *any* cost, it is rather a paying insufficiently; with many it is not a spending of *no* money or of sending *no* soldiers, but it is a committing of less than all (see Luke 14.25–35). Gethsemane is reached by way of the cross. Without the dealing of the cross none can say, "But as thou wilt" (Matt. 26.39). Many are those who aspire to the calling of Abraham but abhor the consecration on Mount Moriah.

Do I fret over my neighbor's easy life? God places me at the bottom of the river to be His overcomer. He allows me to be chained that others may hear the glad tidings. Death works in me, but life in others. This is the only channel of life. The dying of Jesus fills me first with life and then lets this life flow out to others (2 Cor. 4.10–12).

What does God's overcomer do? He stands in the death of Christ that others may receive life. The word of the Bible must be experienced by us first before we are able to preach it. The light of the truth needs first to be transformed into life in us before it can be transmitted as light to others.

God causes His overcomers to see a truth and to prove it in their lives first so that they in turn may bring many to the obedience of this truth. Truth must be organized in us and become a part of our being. Before we can ever tell others about faith, prayer, and consecration, we ourselves must first have the experience of faith, prayer, and consecration. Otherwise, these will merely be terminologies with no substance. God leads us through death so that other people may have life. We are required to go through sufferings and pain before there can be life in others.

For the sake of learning the truth of God, we need first to stand at the bottom of the river. The church is unable to cross over to the mainland for victory because there is a lack of priests standing at the bottom of the river Jordan. All who stand at the bottom of Jordan are capable of creating a seeking heart in others. If a truth has been deeply organized in me, that will draw others to seek the same. Many of the truths of God are waiting to be organized within men. As we let truth be worked into and organized in us, we allow the stature of Christ to grow an inch in us. The overcomers receive life from above to supply the body.

The Selection of the Overcomers

SCRIPTURES TO BE READ:

> And the children of Israel did that which was evil in the sight of Jehovah: and Jehovah delivered them into the hand of Midian seven years. And the hand of Midian

prevailed against Israel; and because of Midian the children of Israel made them the dens which are in the mountains, and the caves, and the strongholds. And so it was, when Israel had sown, that the Midianites came up, and the Amalekites, and the children of the east; they came up against them; and they encamped against them, and destroyed the increase of the earth, till thou come unto Gaza, and left no sustenance in Israel, neither sheep, nor ox, nor ass. For they came up with their cattle and their tents; they came in as locusts for multitude; both they and their camels were without number: and they came into the land to destroy it. And Israel was brought very low because of Midian; and the children of Israel cried unto Jehovah.(Judges 6.1–6)

And he said unto him, Oh, Lord, wherewith shall I save Israel? behold, my family is the poorest in Manasseh, and I am the least in my father's house. And Jehovah said unto him, Surely I will be with thee, and thou shalt smite the Midianites as one man.(Judges 6.15,16)

And Gideon saw that he was the angel of Jehovah; and Gideon said, Alas, O Lord Jehovah! forasmuch as I have seen the angel of Jehovah face to face. And Jehovah said unto him, Peace be unto thee; fear not: thou shalt not die. Then Gideon built an altar there unto Jehovah, and called it Jehovah-Shalom: unto this day it is yet in Ophrah of the Abiezrites.(Judges 6.22–24)

Therefore on that day he called him Jerubbaal, saying, Let Baal contend against him, because he hath broken down his altar.(Judges 6.32)

But the Spirit of Jehovah came upon Gideon; and he blew a trumpet; and Abiezer was gathered together after him. And he sent messengers throughout all Manasseh; and they also were gathered together after him ...(Judges 6.34,35)

And Jehovah said unto Gideon, The people that are with thee are too many for me to give the Midianites into their hand, lest Israel vaunt themselves against me, saying, Mine own hand hath saved me. Now therefore proclaim in the ears of the people, saying, Whosoever is fearful and trembling, let him return and depart from mount Gilead. And there returned of the people twenty and two thousand; and there remained ten thousand. And Jehovah said unto Gideon, The people are yet too many; bring them down unto the water, and I will try them for thee there: and it shall be, that of whom I say unto thee, This shall go with thee, the same shall go with thee; and of whomsoever I say unto thee, This shall not go with thee, the same shall not go. So he brought down the people unto the water: and Jehovah said unto Gideon, Everyone that lappeth of the water with his tongue, as a dog lappeth, him shalt thou set by himself; likewise everyone that boweth down upon his knees to drink. And the number of them that lapped, putting their hand to their mouth, was three hundred men ... And Jehovah said unto Gideon, By the three hundred men that lapped will I save you, and deliver the Midianites into thy hand.(Judges 7.2–7)

So Gideon, and the hundred men that were with him, came unto the outermost part of the camp in the beginning of the middle watch, when they had but newly set the watch: and they blew the trumpets, and brake in pieces the pitchers that were in their hands. And the three companies blew the trumpets, and brake the pitchers, and held the torches in their left hands, and the trumpets in their right hands wherewith to blow; and they cried, The sword of Jehovah and of Gideon. And they stood every man in his place round about the camp; and all the host ran; and they shouted, and put them to flight.(Judges 7.19–21)

And the men of Ephraim said unto him, Why hast thou served us thus, that thou calledst us not, when thou wentest to fight with Midian? And they did chide with him sharply. And he said unto them, What have I now done in comparison with you? Is not the gleaning of the grapes of Ephraim better than the vintage of Abiezer? God hath delivered into your hand the princes of Midian, Oreb and Zeeb: and what was I able to do in comparison with you? Then their anger was abated toward him, when he had said that. And Gideon came to the Jordan, and passed over, he, and the three hundred men that were with him, faint, yet pursuing.(Judges 8.1–4)

We shall now see how the overcomers are selected, and how the overcomers are separated from those who are overcome.

According to the statute in Numbers, all the males of Israel who reached the age of twenty were warriors and able to fight for the Lord. But at the time of the judges, when the children of Israel had failed, God delivered them by choosing 300 men to fight the battle which they all should have fought but were not able so to do. They had failed, and thus were unable to fight for the Lord. A great number of people know how to keep the faith and finish the course but not how to fight the good fight.

How to Become an Overcomer: the Case of Gideon

(1) *Recognize one's own littleness*—that is, know oneself. It is relatively easy to be humble before God; but to be humble before men or to esteem others as more excellent than oneself is extremely difficult. To say I am the least is comparatively easy, but to confess that I am the least in my father's house is not easy. To acknowledge that my father's house is the poorest is not too hard, yet to admit that my father's house is the poorest in Manasseh is most humiliating. He whose face shines and is unconscious of it, though others can see the light of his countenance, is an overcomer. All who look at mirrors in an attempt to see the light on their faces are definitely not overcomers. Although David was anointed, he looked upon himself as a dead dog (1 Sam. 24.14). Overcomers are those who have the reality of, yet not the name of, overcomers.

(2) *See the heavenly vision*—that is, see the Lord. No one without vision is able to serve. With vision, one can press on to reach the goal even though he is beset by difficulties. Having the word of the Lord, one may with certainty sail on to the other shore. The feet of a worker are steadied by the vision he has seen.

(3) *Be not disobedient to the vision*—but respond to the calling of the Lord with sacrifice. One should

offer his insignificant self to God and leave himself in God's hand. Judging one's own self as being either great or small without committing all in God's hand is equally useless. All the living sacrifices according to God's will are accepted by God. Overcomers are called of God. Have you heard the call for overcomers that is found in Revelation chapters 2 and 3? And have you answered the call?

(4) *Break down idols*—which is to say, maintain an outward testimony. A heart already consecrated needs to break down the idols without, in order to bear the testimony. One should pay attention to his own person, his family, and his contacts. Whatever strives to be equal with God must be broken down. He who sees God knows what an idol is. Having seen the angel of the Lord—that is to say, the Lord himself, one discerns the things outside the Lord as idols. A sight of the angel of the Lord reveals the wood (the Asherah) as not being God (Judges 6.22–27). The sacrifice on the rock is for a personal purpose, whereas the sacrifice on the altar is for corporate use.

After these four steps have been taken, the Holy Spirit will fall on the person. The filling of the Holy Spirit is not the result of asking for power; when one stands on the right ground, he shall receive the outpoured Spirit.

A blowing of the trumpet is a calling the people to join in as overcomers. Independent action is not appropriate to an overcomer. We should purify ourselves from those who have been overcome, but must not be separated from the other overcomers.

How to Select Overcomers: the Case of the 300

(1) *The first selection*—the result of which 22,000 left. Why? Because (a) they intended to glorify themselves. Sometimes we are willing to sacrifice life but not glory. We must overcome ourselves as well as Satan. God seeks people who will work for Him without bragging about their work. After we have labored we should say, "I am an unprofitable servant"(see Luke 17.10). We need to forget how many fields we have ploughed and how many sheep we have watched. God cannot share His glory with us. If we secretly expect something for ourselves we will be among the eliminated.

And (b) they were fearful and trembling. Whoever is fearful and trembling may as well go home. It is essential that we do not love ourselves and are ready to endure sufferings. The greatest afflictions are not material in nature but spiritual. All who seek to glorify themselves and are fearful and trembling will be eliminated. Victory lies not in number but in knowing God.

(2) *The second selection*—the test for which lay in the tiny matter of drinking water. Small things frequently reveal our real situation. In those days both the Jews and Arabs travelled with their baggage on their backs. There were therefore two different ways to drink water while on the road: (a) by unloading the baggage and bowing down upon their knees to drink, or (b) by lapping water from their hands for the sake of hurrying up their journey on the road and of guarding against plunderers. Of the ten thousand men left,

9,700 knelt down to drink; only 300 lapped up the water from their hands. All those who bowed to drink were eliminated by God. Only those who drank from their hands were chosen. Whoever has opportunity to indulge and yet refrains from doing so has known the dealing of the cross. Such persons will be used of God. Ever ready to let the cross work in his life, this is the man whom God will use.

Hence the three qualifications in God's selection of overcomers are: (1) they must be wholly for the glory of God; (2) they must be fearful of nothing, and (3) they must allow the cross to deal with self. We ourselves may decide whether or not we will be overcomers. When God tests us, our real selves will be revealed—thus telling us if we are overcomers. He who knows the victory of the cross in his life is able to maintain the victory of the cross continuously.

The Victory of the Overcomers

God gave 300 men to Gideon and caused them to be one body. It is highly irregular to overcome unrelatedly. Gideon and the 300 acted in concert. This was possible since their flesh had been cut off. This is the unity of the Holy Spirit and life in the body. The records in the New Testament relate especially to meetings, not to works.

The Outcome

The 300 fought the battle, and all the children of Israel came out to chase the enemies. The 300 labored, and the whole nation reaped. We overcome, and the whole body revives. Standing in the bottom of the river is not for ourselves but is for the entire church: "Now I rejoice in my sufferings for your sake, and fill up on my part that which is lacking of the afflictions of Christ in my flesh for his body's sake, which is the church" (Col. 1.24). Overcomers will be upbraided by others just as Gideon was chided by the men of Ephraim. Gideon defeated not only the Midianites on the outside but also the Midianites on the inside! Only such could continue to overcome, just as the record indicates: "Faint, yet pursuing" (Judges 8.4).

The Prayer of the Overcomers

SCRIPTURES TO BE READ:

Verily I say unto you, What things soever ye shall bind on earth shall be bound in heaven; and what things soever ye shall loose on earth shall be loosed in heaven.(Matt. 18.18)

For our wrestling is not against flesh and blood, but against the principalities, against the powers, against the world-rulers of this darkness, against the spiritual hosts of wickedness in the heavenly places. Wherefore take up the whole armour of God, that ye may be able to withstand in the evil day, and, having done all, to stand.(Eph. 6. 12,13—especially the word *Wherefore*)

And what the exceeding greatness of his power to us-ward who believe, according to that working of the strength of his might which he wrought in Christ, when he raised him from the dead, and made him to sit at his right hand in the heavenly places, far above all rule, and authority, and power, and dominion, and every name that is named, not only in this world, but also in that which is to come: and he put all things in subjection under his feet, and gave him to be head over all things to the church.(Eph. 1.19–22)

And raised us up with him, and made us to sit with him in the heavenly places, in Christ Jesus.(Eph. 2.6)

Verily I say unto you, Whoseover shall say unto this mountain, Be thou taken up and cast into the sea; and shall not doubt in his heart, but shall believe that what he saith cometh to pass; he shall have it. Therefore I say unto you, All things whatsoever ye pray and ask for, believe that ye received them, and ye shall have them.(Mark 11.23,24 mg.)

Authoritative Prayer

God's overcomers must learn how to use the authority of Christ and pray authoritative prayer. Prayer in the Scriptures is not only an asking but even more so an expression of authority. Command with authority—such is prayer.

Hence God's overcomers must on the one hand be faithful in denying their own selves, the world, and Satan; but on the other hand know how to exercise the authority of Christ. We should (1) let God defeat us with the cross so that we may be defeated before God, and (2) defeat Satan by using the authority of Christ so that we may win the victory over Satan. Authoritative prayer is not petitioning, it is commanding; for there are *two* kinds of prayer: not only the prayer of petition but also the prayer of command: "Command ye me" says Isaiah 45.11. We may command God to do things, and such is commanding prayer.

Commanding prayer commences at the ascension of Christ. The death and resurrection of Christ, as we have seen, resolves God's four cardinal issues—so that His death concludes all that is in Adam, His resurrection gives us new ground, and His ascension makes us sit in the heavenly places far above all rule and authority and power and dominion and every name that is named: not only in this world but also in that which is to come. Ephesians 1 is a record of the ascension of Christ who ascended far above all rule and authority. Ephesians 2 tells of our sitting with Christ in the heavenly places. As Christ is far above all rule and authority, so we also are above all rule and authority.

Ephesians 1 tells us that the position of Christ is in the heavenly places. Chapter 2 tells us that our place in Christ is sitting with Him in the heavenly places. Chapter 6 tells us what we do in the heavenly places, even sitting there and praying—that is to say, exercising the authority of Christ and giving out commanding prayers. Ordinary prayer is a praying from earth to heaven. Commanding prayer is a praying from heaven to earth. The prayer in Matthew 6 is petitionary prayer, and hence is upward in direction. The prayer in Ephesians 6 is commanding prayer, and therefore it is downward. Thus we sit in the heavenly places and pour forth commanding prayer. "Amen" in Hebrew means "So be it" or "So it is"—this is command. At the beginning of any warfare Satan tries to unseat us from our heavenly position, which is one of victory. Warfare is a battle for position. Hence victory lies in occupying the right place. Being in Christ and sitting in the heavenly places alone gives authoritative prayer.

The "therefore" in Mark 11.24 shows us that verse 23 also deals with the subject of prayer. Yet nowhere in verse 23 are we told to pray to God. Instead it simply says, "Say unto this mountain"—that is, it is a commanding the mountain. A not speaking to God is also prayer—authoritative prayer. It is not asking *God* to deal with the mountain, the latter of which represents things that hinder. Only with perfect faith may one speak to the *mountain.* Now perfect faith comes out of perfect knowledge of God's will. And thus we command what God has already commanded; we decide on that which God has already decided. Due to the fact of fully knowing God's will, such faith as this is possible.

The Relationship between Authoritative Prayer and Overcomers

He who sits on the throne is God the Lord. He who succumbs beneath the throne is the Enemy. Prayer links us with God. All who overcome and reign as kings know how to pray. They know how to exercise the authority of God's throne (for this authority rules the universe). We may turn to the throne and use the authority therein to bring a brother to us (Hudson Taylor, to cite one example, had exercised such authority). For the overcomers to rule over the church, the world, and even the powers of the air, they must rely on the authority of the throne. Once about ten years ago some brethren in England wielded this authority of the throne to control political change. This is a reigning over the nations. Spiritual warfare is offensive as well as defensive in nature. The control is not only over the nations but also over Hades and its principalities, authorities, powers, and dominions. May God teach us how to use the authority of Christ, because all things are in subjection under His feet since He is the Head of the church. And if we use the authority of God, we may bring all things under our feet too.

Matthew 18.18,19 deals with prayer. From the phrases "on earth" and "in heaven" of verse 19 we understand that the prayer in verse 18 is commanding prayer. For this prayer is action, not petition. It is a binding, not an asking God to bind. This commanding prayer has two aspects about it:

(1) *Bind*—bind all the inordinate activities of the brothers and sisters in the meeting; bind all the disturbances to the work that come from people of the world; bind all the evil spirits and demons; and bind Satan and all his activities. We may rule as kings over all things. Whenever a thing happens in the world or among the brethren, that is the moment for us to rule as kings.

(2) *Loose*—we may also loose people. Loose all the timid brethren; loose all who ought to come out and work for the Lord; loose money in the grip of people that it might be given for God's use; and loose the truths of God.

We are ambassadors of God, and therefore we enjoy extraterritoriality on earth. We may call in heaven to rule over the earth.

Things God's Overcomers Ought to Do in the End Time

SCRIPTURES TO BE READ:

And Jehovah God said unto the serpent, Because thou hast done this, cursed art thou above all cattle, and above every beast of the field; upon thy belly shalt thou go, and dust shalt thou eat all the days of thy life: and I will put enmity between thee and the woman, and between thy seed and her seed: he shall bruise thy head, and thou shalt bruise his heel.(Gen. 3.14,15)

And a great sign was seen in heaven: a woman arrayed with the sun, and the moon under her feet, and upon her head a crown of twelve stars; and she was with child; and she crieth out, travailing in birth, and in pain to be delivered. And there was seen another sign in heaven: and behold, a great red dragon, having seven heads and ten horns, and upon his heads seven diadems. And his tail draweth the third part of the stars of heaven, and did cast them to the earth: and the dragon standeth before the woman that is about to be delivered, that when she is delivered he may devour her child. And she was delivered of a son, a man child, who is to rule all the nations with a rod of iron: and her child was caught up unto God, and unto his throne ... And the great dragon was cast down, the old serpent, he that is called the Devil and Satan, the deceiver of the whole world; he was cast down to the earth, and his angels were cast down with him. And I heard a great voice in heaven, saying, Now is come the salvation, and the power, and the kingdom of our God, and the authority of his Christ: for the accuser of our brethren is cast down, who accuseth them before our God day and night. And they overcame him because of the blood of the Lamb, and because of the word of their testimony; and they loved not their life even unto death.(Rev. 12.1–11)

These two passages of Scripture respond to each other. The first one is found in the opening book of the Bible, while the next one is in the closing book of the Bible. In Genesis 3 there are (1) the serpent, (2) the woman, and (3) the seed in view. In Revelation 12 there are again these three: (1) the serpent, (2) the woman, and (3) the man child.

God's Judgment against the Serpent

Genesis 3 reveals God's judgment against Satan. It also tells us of His judgment against fallen man as well as of His plan of redemption. "Upon thy belly shalt thou go" is God's decision that Satan can only work on earth, no longer can he work in the universe. "Dust shalt thou eat all the days of thy life" suggests that God has ordained that henceforth man (man of the dust) shall be Satan's food. Thus all the descendants of Adam, as God has ruled, become food—that is to say, they are a people—for Satan.

"Woman" refers to the mother of all living. Hence she represents all living: all whom God desires to save.

"Her seed" refers to Christ. When Christ was on earth He crushed the serpent's head on the cross. Since in the head lies the vital region of power, the Lord has broken all the principal powers belonging to Satan.

For the Bible to say that the serpent is to bruise the heel of the woman's seed is simply to denote that Satan will work behind the back of Christ. After Christ has bruised the serpent's head and left, Satan works behind His back. This means that he works on the lives of the believers in Christ—and such is a behind-the-scenes sort of work.

The woman's seed points to the corporate Christ as well as to the personal Christ, since all who have part in the resurrection of Christ are included in the seed of the woman. As our Lord was born of a woman without the help of a man, so the new man who is reborn in a believer does not have the Adamic nature. As Christ is the Son of God, so the new man is also a son of God. As Christ was not born of blood, so the new man is not born of blood nor of the will of man (John 1.12,13).

From Genesis 3 onward, the hope of both God and man centers on the seed of the woman. Satan too pays great attention to the seed of the woman. For this very reason he (1) instigated Herod to kill the Lord, (2) tempted the Lord in the wilderness, and (3) tried to harass the Lord throughout the three and a half years of His public ministry. But in all these the Lord was victorious.

The Overcomers Deal with the Serpent

Narratively, Revelation 4–11 is one section, 15–22 is another. Chapters 12–14 are parenthetical; these do not belong to the main text but serve to explain what has been written before. In thought, chapter 12 is linked with chapters 2 and 3: for note that chapters 2 and 3 mention "he that overcometh" seven times and then chapter 12 says "they overcame him"; chapters 2 and 3 tell us how God calls for some to be overcomers when the church has generally failed, while chapter 12 shows us who are these overcomers and what they do; and again, 2.27 relates how the overcomer shall rule the nations with a rod of iron and 12.5 confirms that he who shall rule the nations with a rod of iron is the man child. The man child represents the overcomers in the church. This man child is corporate in nature, because he is the brethren spoken of in 12.10,11.

"The old serpent" is the name God purposely mentions here in Revelation 12 to help us recall the record in Genesis 3.

The woman who gives birth to the man child as

spoken of in Revelation 12 is Jerusalem. It refers not just to the earthly Jerusalem, it also points to the heavenly Jerusalem. The Bible tells us that God is our Father, the Lord is our older brother, and Jerusalem is our mother (Gal. 4.26).

The sun, moon, and twelve stars coincide with Joseph's dream. Hence this must allude to the children of Israel. Jerusalem is the center of the nation of Israel. Consequently the woman should be Jerusalem.

The woman is the Jerusalem of Revelation 21 and 22. This city includes all who have the life of Christ and are saved during both the Old and the New Testament times. Before she gives birth to the man child the woman represents the church; after she has brought forth the man child she stands for the children of Israel: because before the man child is born she is described in her heavenly state—the sun, moon, and stars, whereas after the man child is born she is spoken of in her earthly situation—she is fleeing into the wilderness.

The woman symbolizes all the redeemed of God. They are severely persecuted by the Enemy. How the woman suffers from the serpent! These who are represented by the woman ought to fight for themselves, yet they cannot. So God calls from among them a company of overcomers to fight the battle for them. These overcomers shall rule the nations with a rod of iron since they will occupy a special place in the kingdom. As these overcomers (as represented by the man child) are caught up to heaven, they cast down Satan and regain the heavenly places from the serpent.

When they are on earth, Satan has to retreat; and when they ascend to heaven, Satan is cast down. Victory lies in regaining the ground. The man child conquers on behalf of the mother: the overcomers win the victory for the church. Moreover, in the end time, God uses overcomers to conclude the war in heaven. These overcomers shall bring "the salvation, and the power, and the kingdom of our God, and the authority of his Christ" into heaven. The serpent therefore has no more place in heaven. Hence wherever the overcomers are, Satan is forced to retreat.

The Arms of the Overcomers

They overcome the Enemy because of: (1) "The blood of the Lamb"—*First*, in the blood of Christ the natural life is poured forth; hence Satan can no longer work in us. Satan's food is the dust of the earth: he can only work in natural life. *Second,* the blood of Christ overcomes the attack of Satan. Under the protection of the blood of Christ we will not be attacked by him, just as the children of Israel were fully protected by the blood of the Paschal Lamb. The blood satisfies the righteousness of God, because the shedding of blood signifies death. For this reason, Satan cannot attack us. *Third,* the blood of Christ answers the accusations of the Enemy.

(2) "The word of their testimony"—What the Enemy tries to do to the church is to overturn the testimony. The church is a lampstand, which symbolizes testimony. In order to overthrow the church Satan has to overturn the testimony. The testimony mentioned here

is especially related to the testimony given against Satan. Three words which our Lord used while tempted himself form the testimony to be used against him. We should testify against the Enemy. When he tells us we are weak, we tell him that Christ's "power is made perfect in weakness" (2 Cor. 12.9). Use the word of God to implement the victory of Christ. The blood stands for such victory. Using the word of God to execute the victory of Christ is testimony.

(3) "Loved not their life even unto death"—Offer up our body and life, have no self-pity and, like Paul, "hold not (your) life of any account as dear unto (yourself)" (Acts 20.24). The battle shall be won if we trust in the blood, give the word of testimony boldly, and maintain an attitude of no fear of death. Such people can fulfill the determinate will of God recorded in Genesis 3.15.

As the dragon waits to devour the man child about to be delivered, so Satan will now persecute and cause us to suffer. But these very persecutions and sufferings will impel us to be the man child so that we may be raptured first. The first rapture is not only a blessing, it also entails a responsibility. All who give ground in their hearts to Satan will be persecuted by the dragon in the Great Tribulation. But those in whose hearts the Enemy has no foothold shall bruise the head of the dragon under their feet (cf. Rom. 16.20). Because the serpent has injured the woman, it takes the seed of the woman to defeat the serpent. God himself does not come to defeat Satan. He calls overcomers to defeat him. May we be among the ranks of the overcomers!

TITLES YOU
WILL WANT TO HAVE

By Watchman Nee

CD ROM – Complete works of Nee by CFP

Basic Lesson Series
Volume 1 – A Living Sacrifice
Volume 2 – The Good Confession
Volume 3 – Assembling Together
Volume 4- Not I, But Christ
Volume 5 – Do All to the Glory of God
Volume 6 – Love One Another

The Church and the Work
Volume 1 – Assembly Life
Volume 2 – Rethinking the Work
Volume 3 – Church Affairs
Revive Thy Work
The Word of the Cross
The Communion of the Holy Spirit
The Finest of the Wheat – Volume 1
The Finest of the Wheat – Volume 2
Take Heed
Worship God
Interpreting Matthew
The Character of God's Workman
Gleanings in the Fields of Boaz
The Spirit of the Gospel
The life That Wins
From Glory to Glory
The Spirit of Judgment
From Faith to Faith
Back to the Cross
The Lord My Portion
Aids to "Revelation"
Grace for Grace
The Better Covenant
A Balanced Christian Life
The Mystery of Creation

The Messenger of the Cross
Full of Grace and Truth – Volume 1
Full of Grace and Truth – Volume 2
The Spirit of Wisdom and Revelation
Whom Shall I Send?
The Testimony of God
The Salvation of the Soul
The King and the Kingdom of Heaven
The Body of Christ: A Reality
Let Us Pray
God's Plan and the Overcomers
The Glory of His Life
"Come, Lord Jesus"
Practical Issues of This Life
Gospel Dialogue
God's Work
Ye Search the Scriptures
The Prayer Ministry of the Church
Christ the Sum of All Spiritual Things
Spiritual Knowledge
The Latent Power of the Soul
The Ministry of God's Word
Spiritual Reality or Obsession
The Spiritual Man
The Release of The Spirit
Spiritual Authority

By Stephen Kaung

Discipled to Christ
The Splendor of His Ways
Seeing the Lord's End in Job
The Songs of Degrees
Meditations on Fifteen Psalms

ORDER FROM:

Christian Fellowship Publishers, Inc.
11515 Allecingie Parkway
Richmond, Virginia 23235